I0488558

Vintage Christmas

an Adult Coloring Book

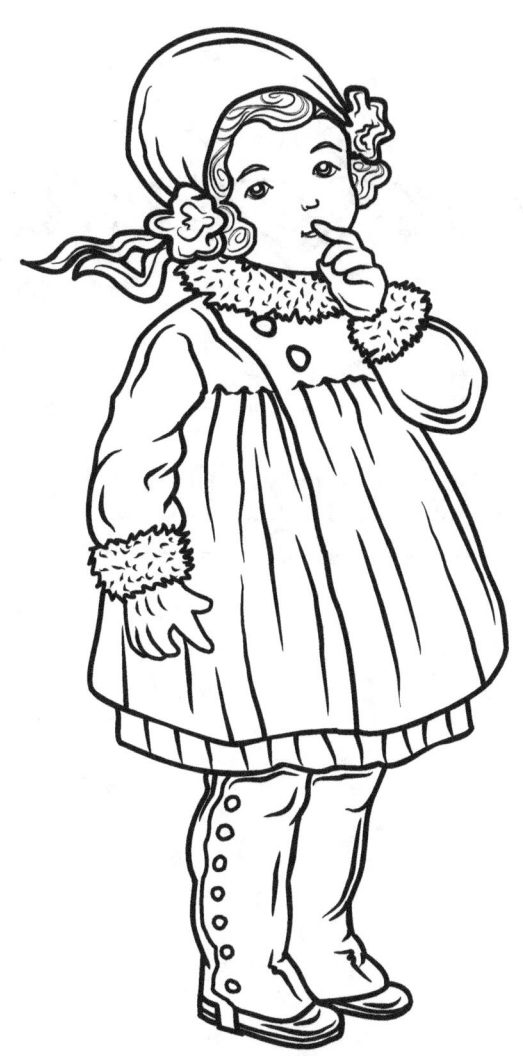

by Tes Scholtz

Artwork Anywhere™

COLOR THIS!
YOURS COULD BE OUR NEW FACEBOOK COVER PHOTO!
GET MORE INFO AND DOWNLOAD PRINTABLE COPIES AT
ARTWORKANYWHERE.COM/FB

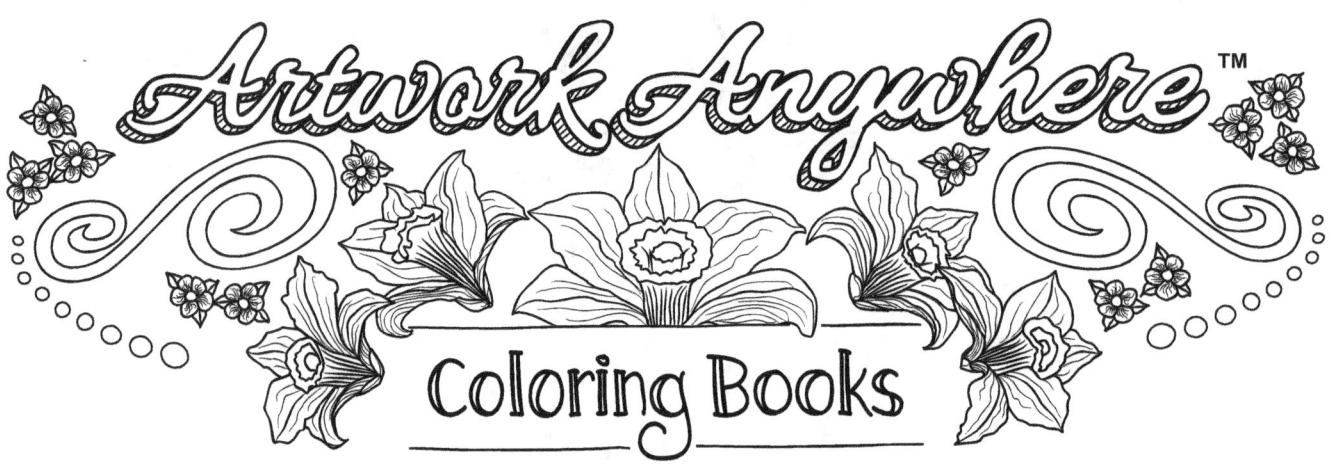

Cover: The front and back cover were designed and colored by Tes Scholtz.
Hand coloring was done with Spectrum Noir™ markers.

Vintage Christmas
an Adult Coloring Book

by Tes Scholtz

Artwork Anywhere ™

Vintage Christmas adult coloring book features 25 hand drawn illustrations celebrating the feeling of an old-fashioned Christmas. Holly, mistletoe, ribbons, and bells adorn pages filled with snowy scenes, winter birds, warm little children and of course, Santa!

"I really loved drawing this book, and hope it fills you with warmth and wonder." ~Tes

Use colored pencils, crayons, inks, gel pens, markers, whatever you want, or mix it up and use them all! There are no rules. There are suggestions, though: Some markers and paints may bleed through the pages. To avoid damaging other pages, use a barrier sheet between pages, or remove the page from the book before coloring.

All of my coloring books are printed single-sided, so you don't have to worry about colors showing through the back side, or smudging against each other face-to-face. Plus, no more deciding which side you like better if you want to remove it from the book.
Each page is meant to be enjoyed on its own.

 *ArtworkAnywhere.com*

Be sure to check out ArtworkAnywhere.com for our latest coloring books, plus updates, contests, and exclusive free coloring pages!

We love to see your work! Please share your favorite colorings, so we can show it off!
Visit ArtworkAnywhere.com/social to see where we are on social media.

Do you have questions, criticism, compliments, ideas? Send your thoughts to:
suggestions@artworkanywhere.com

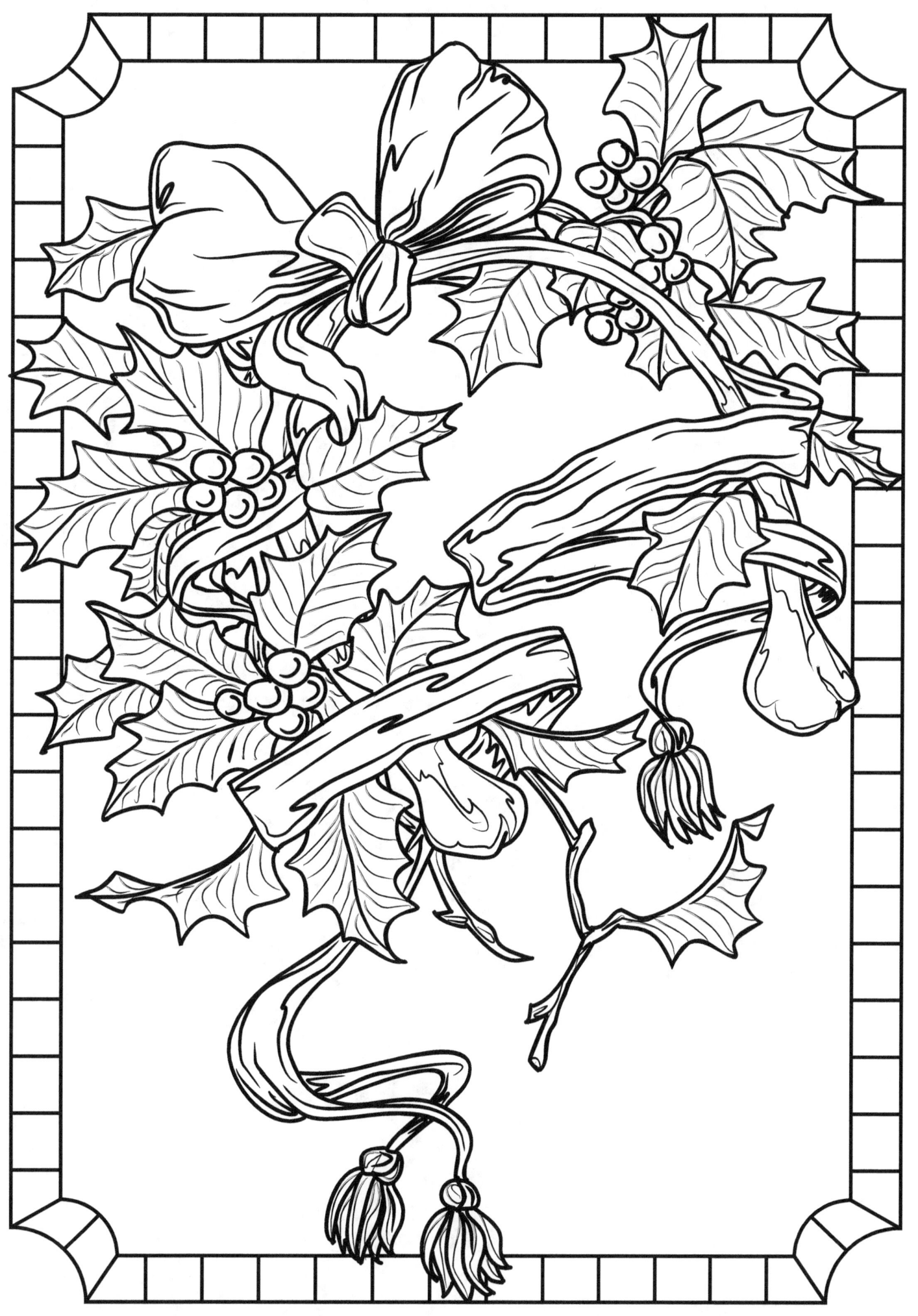

ArtworkAnywhere.com

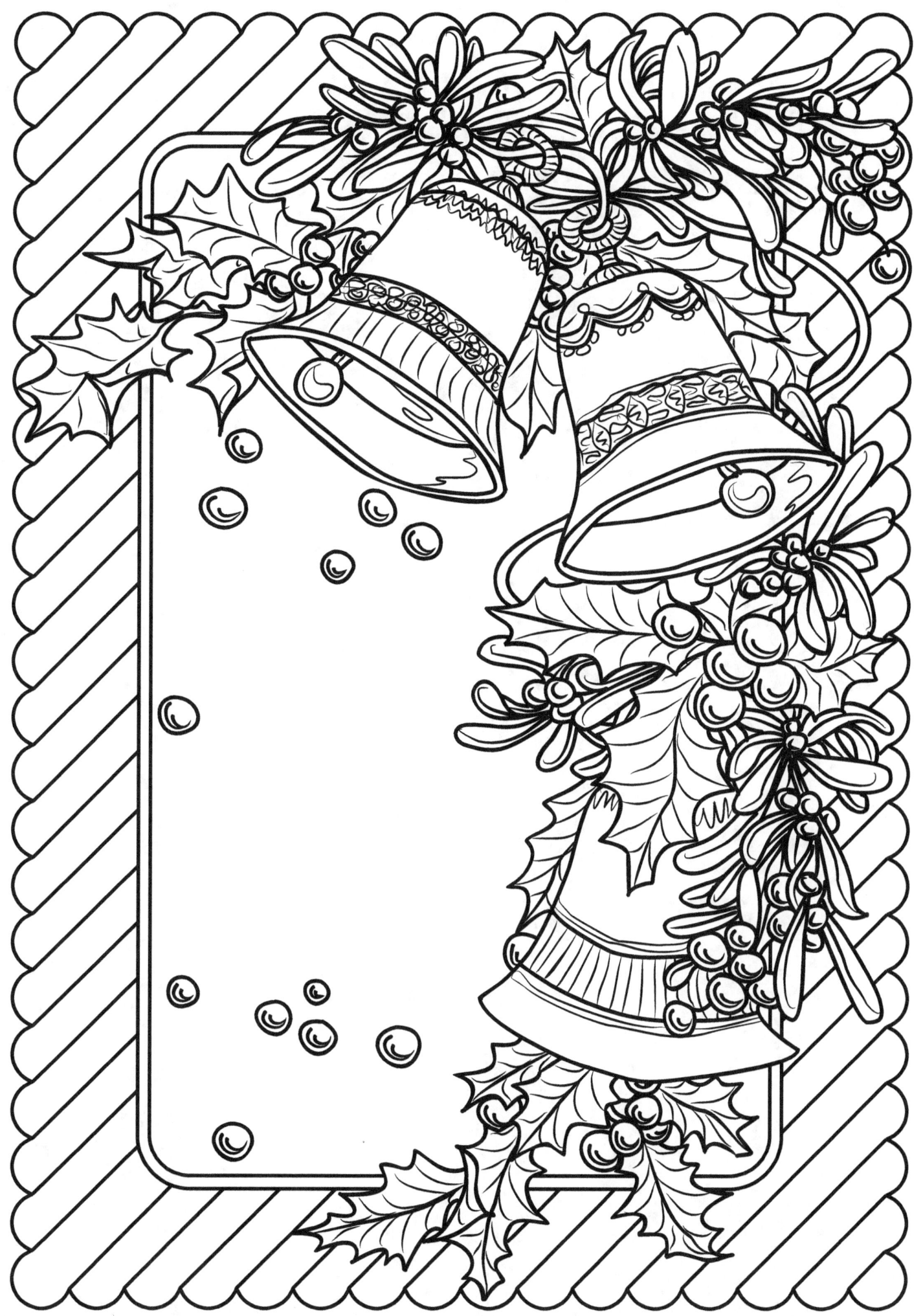

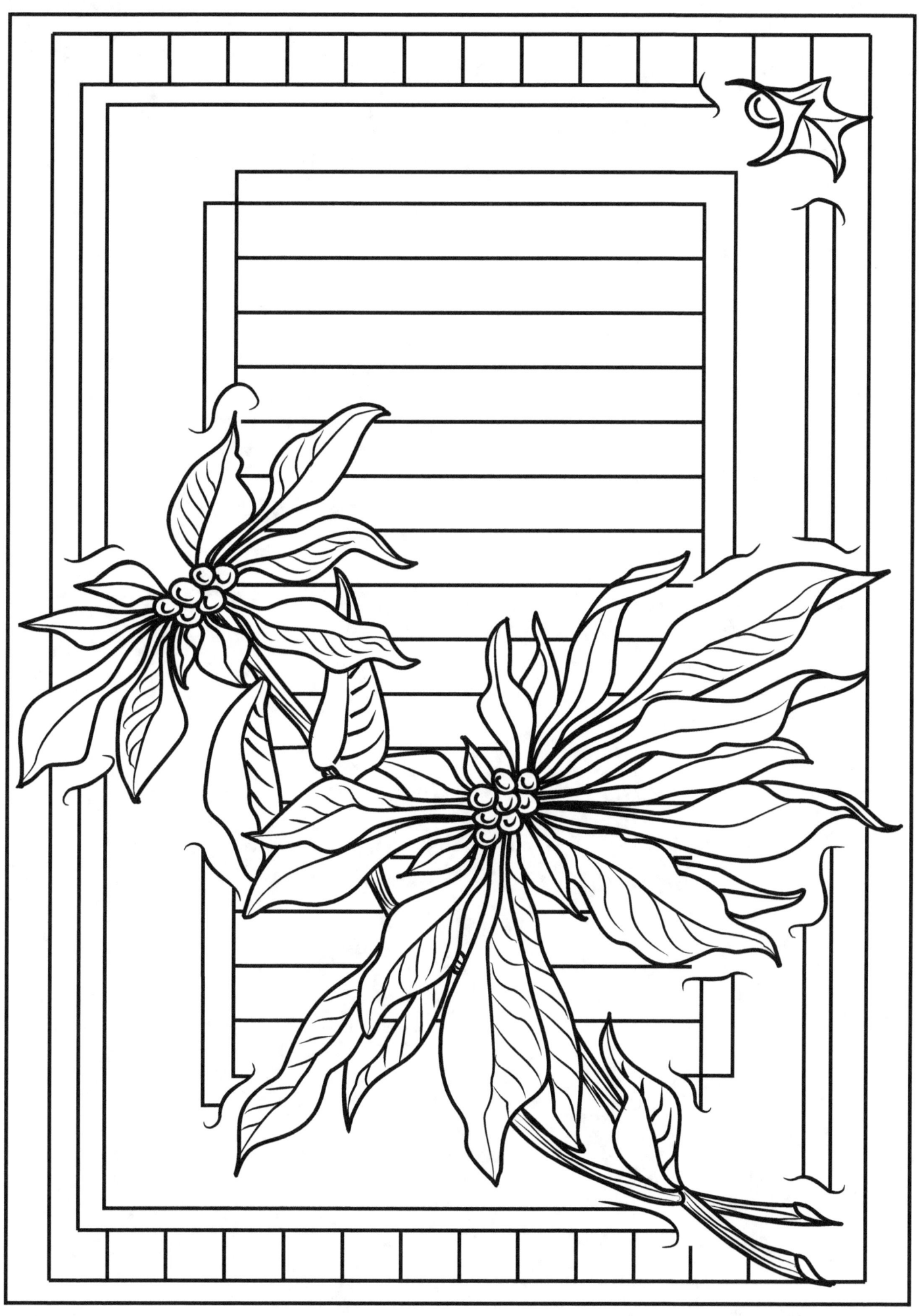

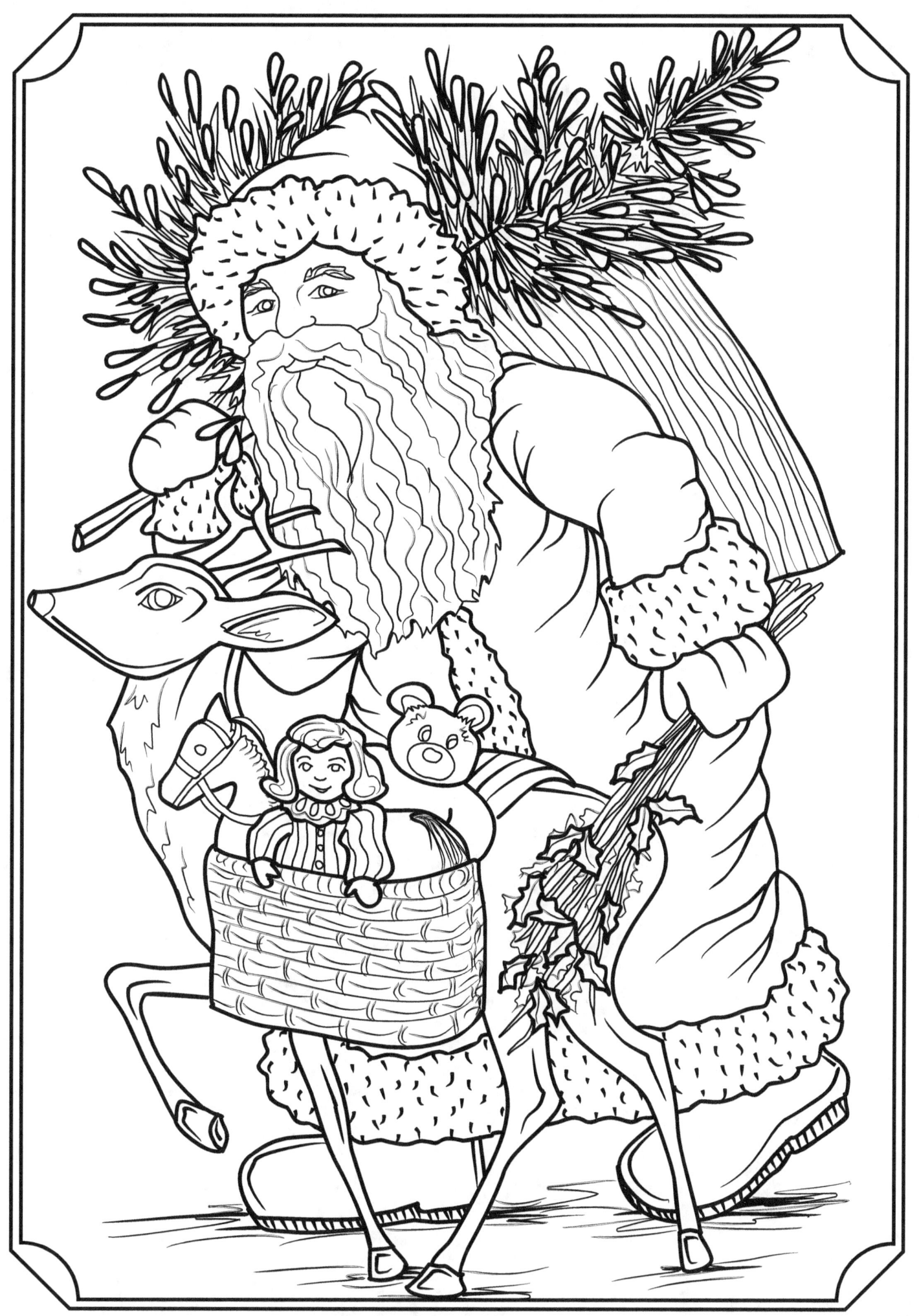

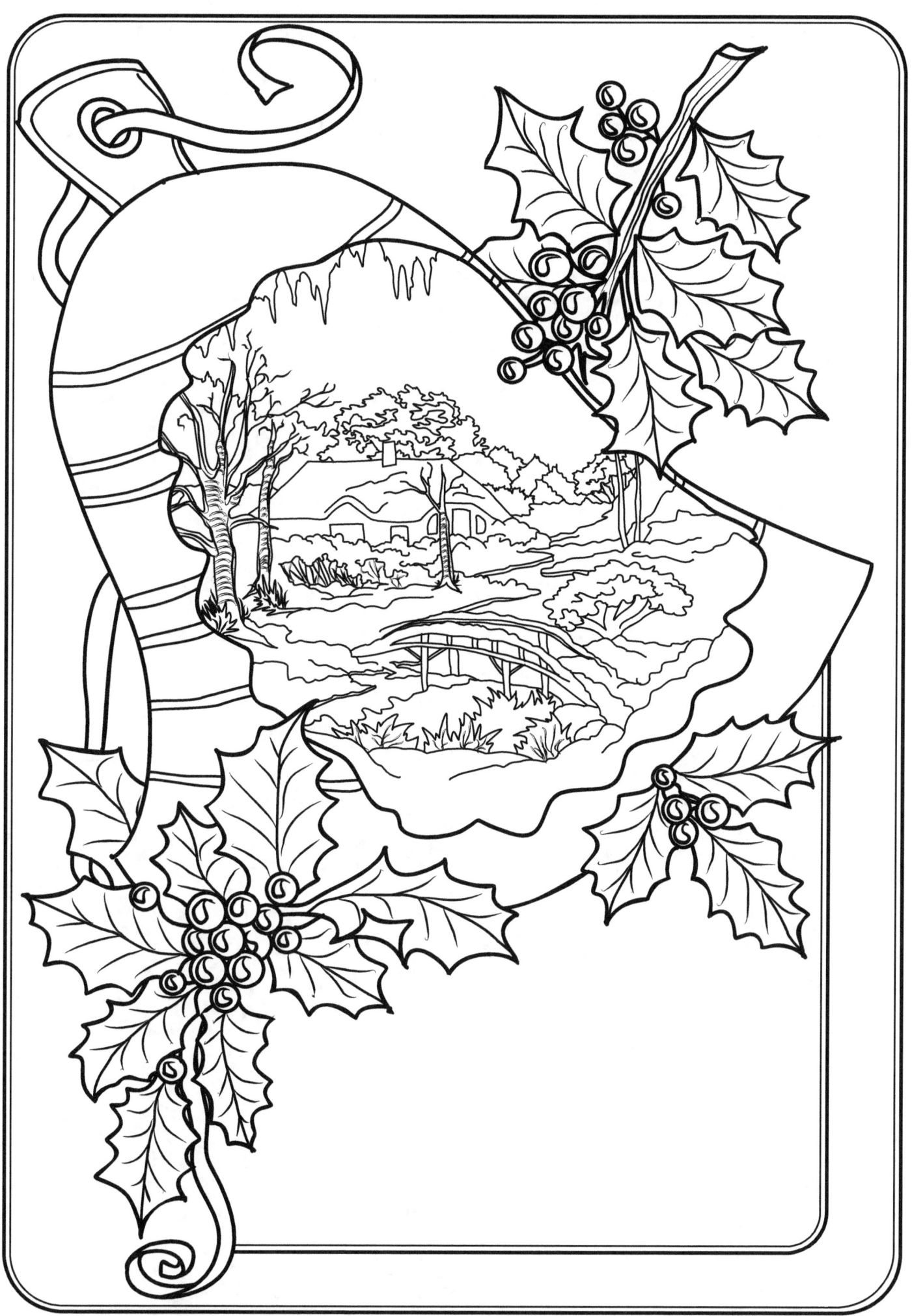

ArtworkAnywhere.com

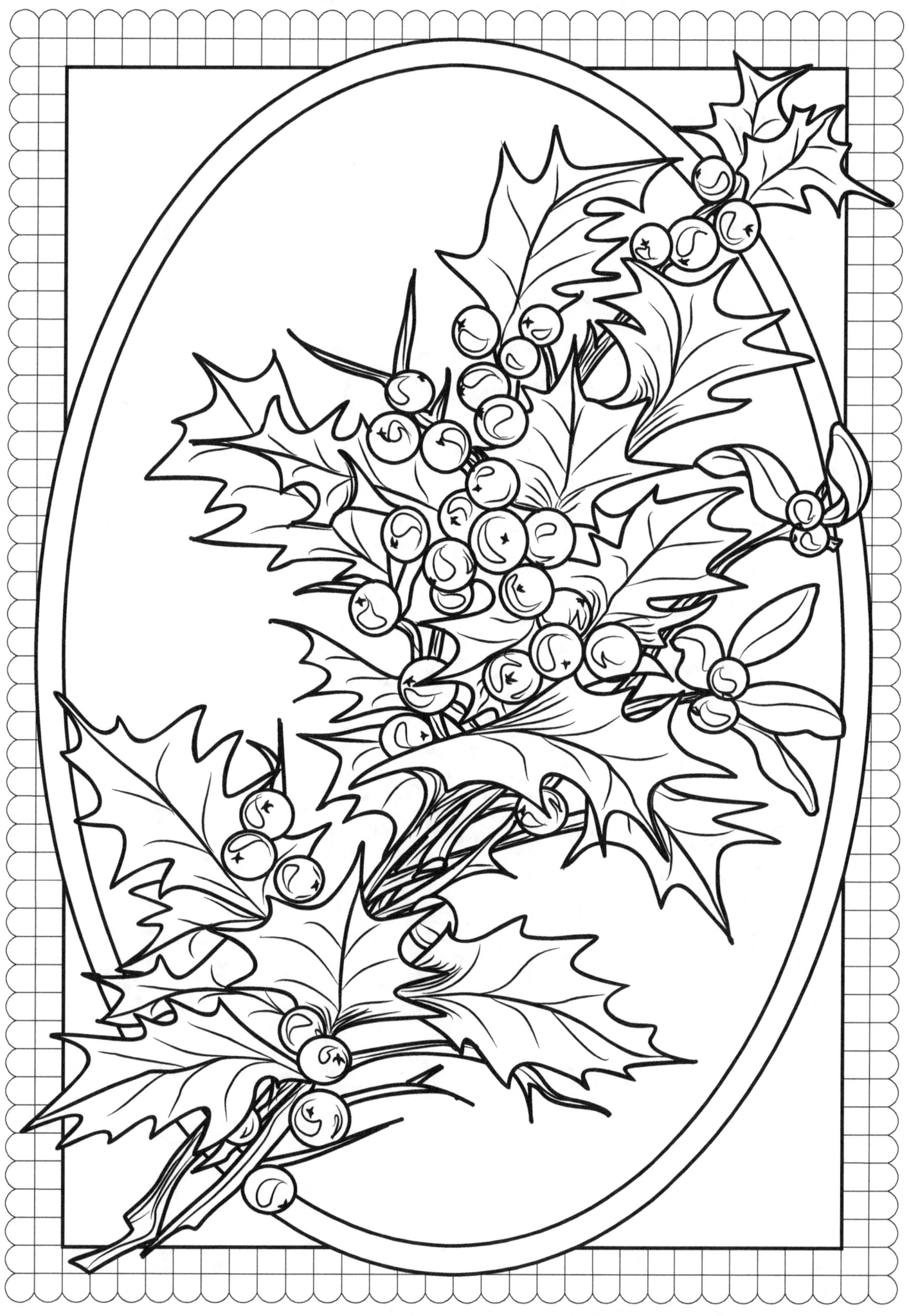

ArtworkAnywhere.com

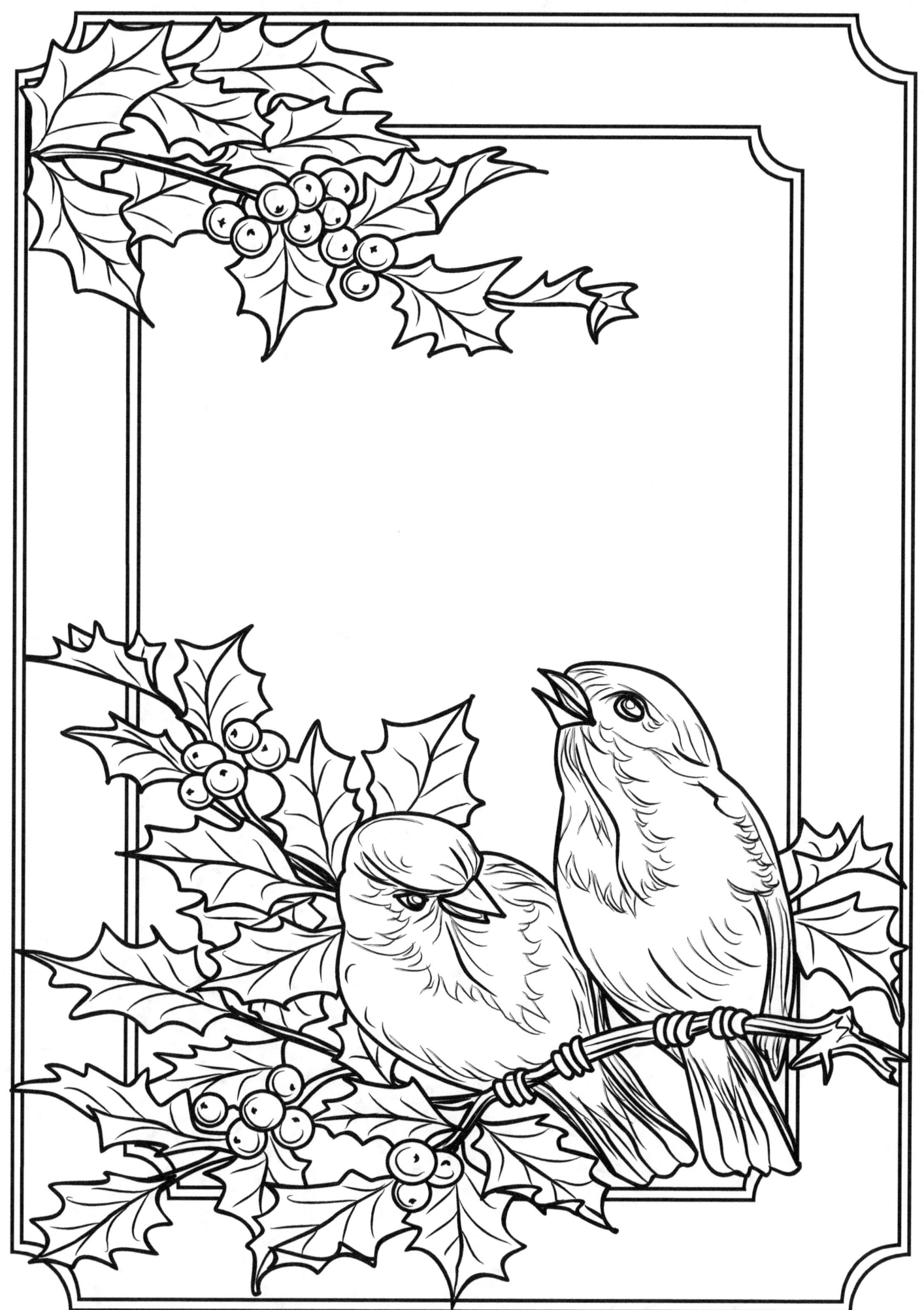

ArtworkAnywhere.com

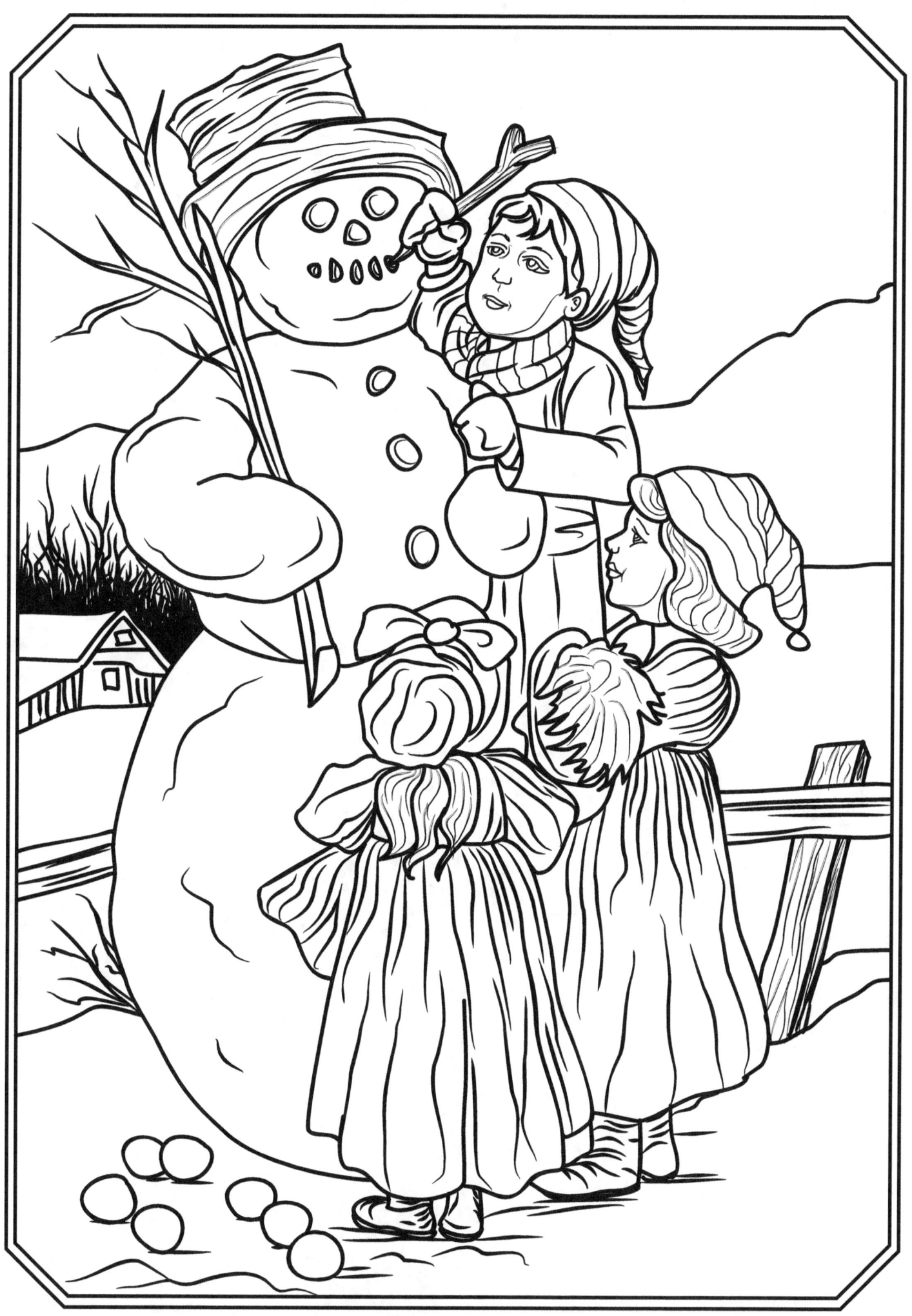

ArtworkAnywhere.com

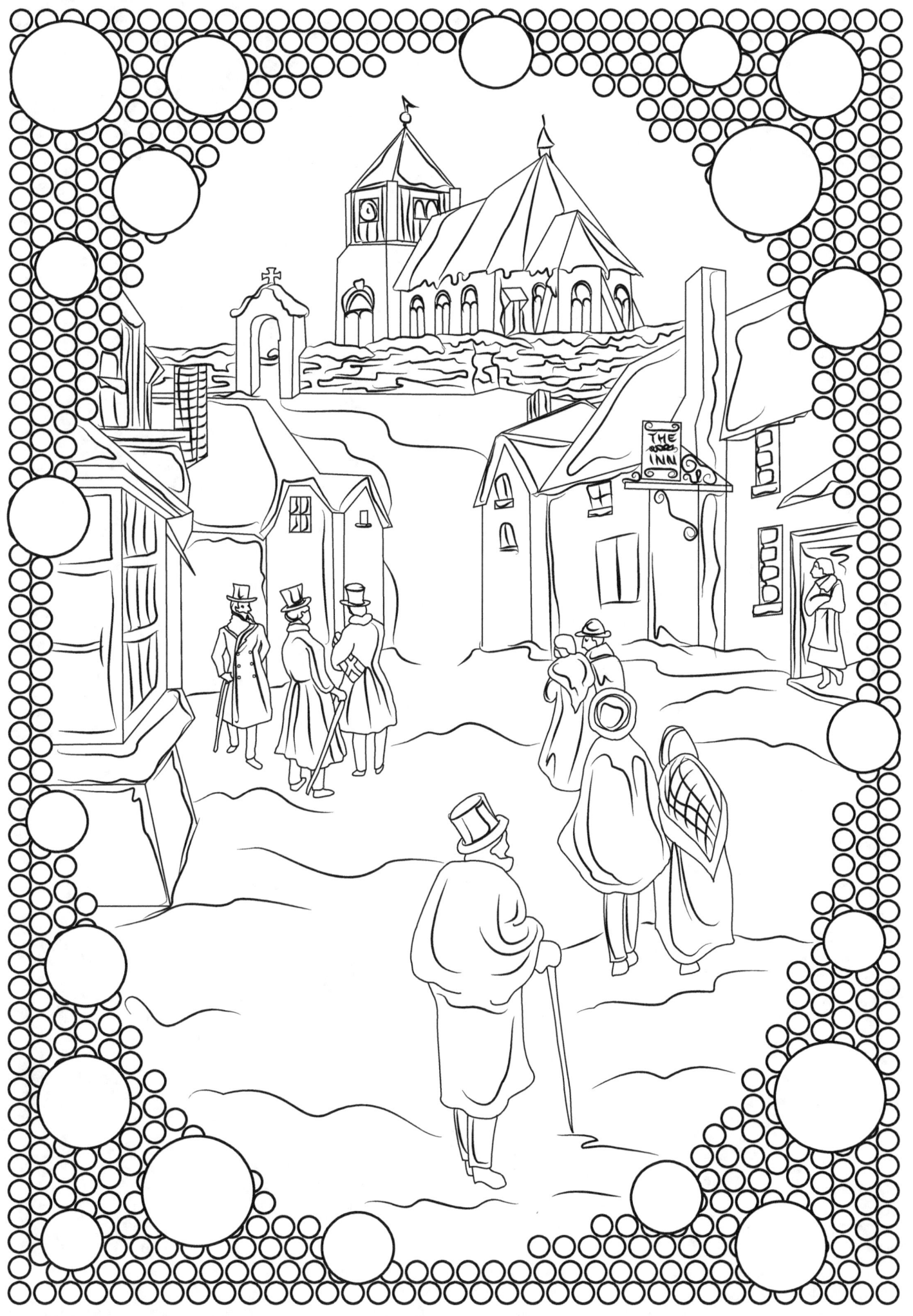

ArtworkAnywhere.com

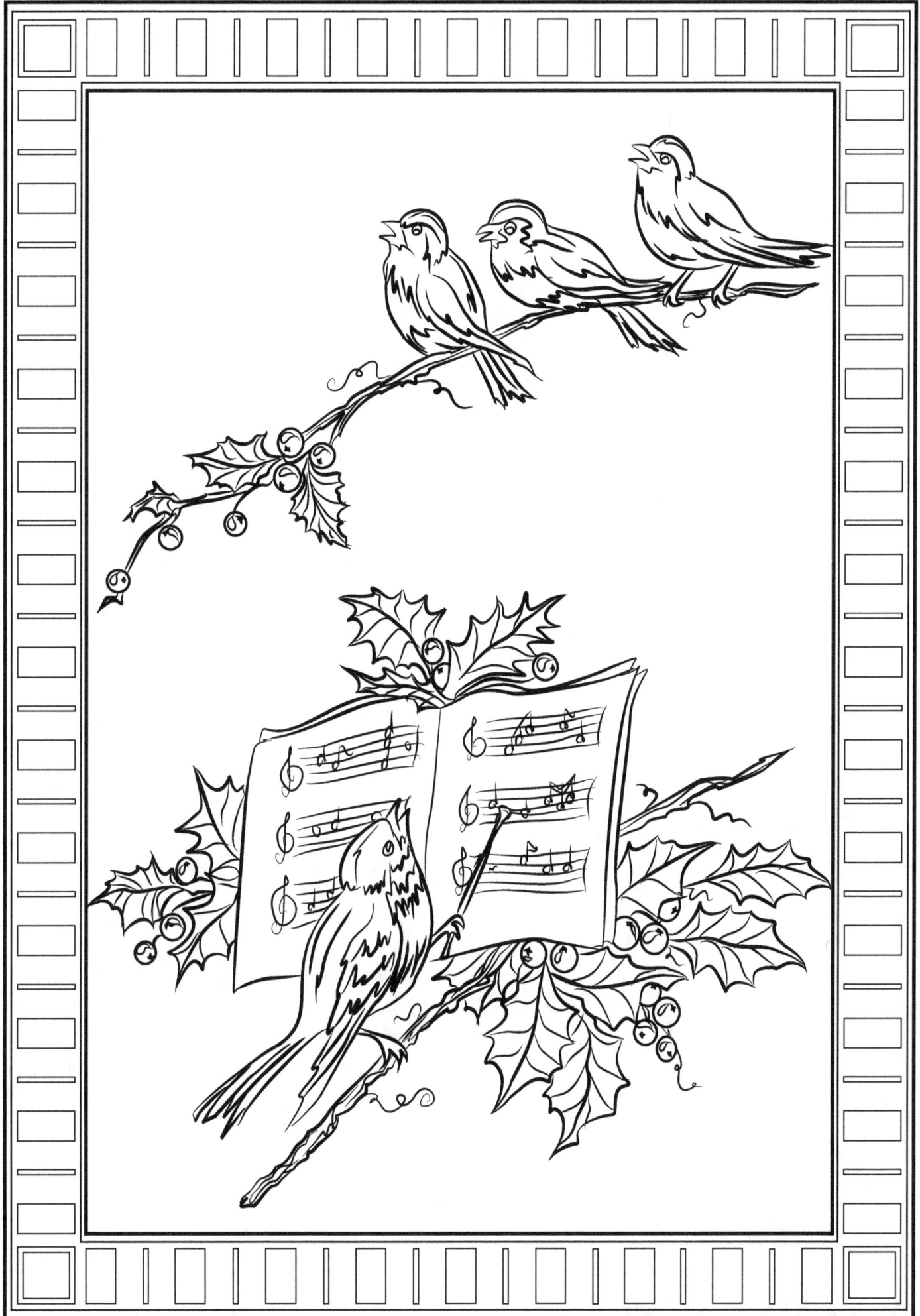

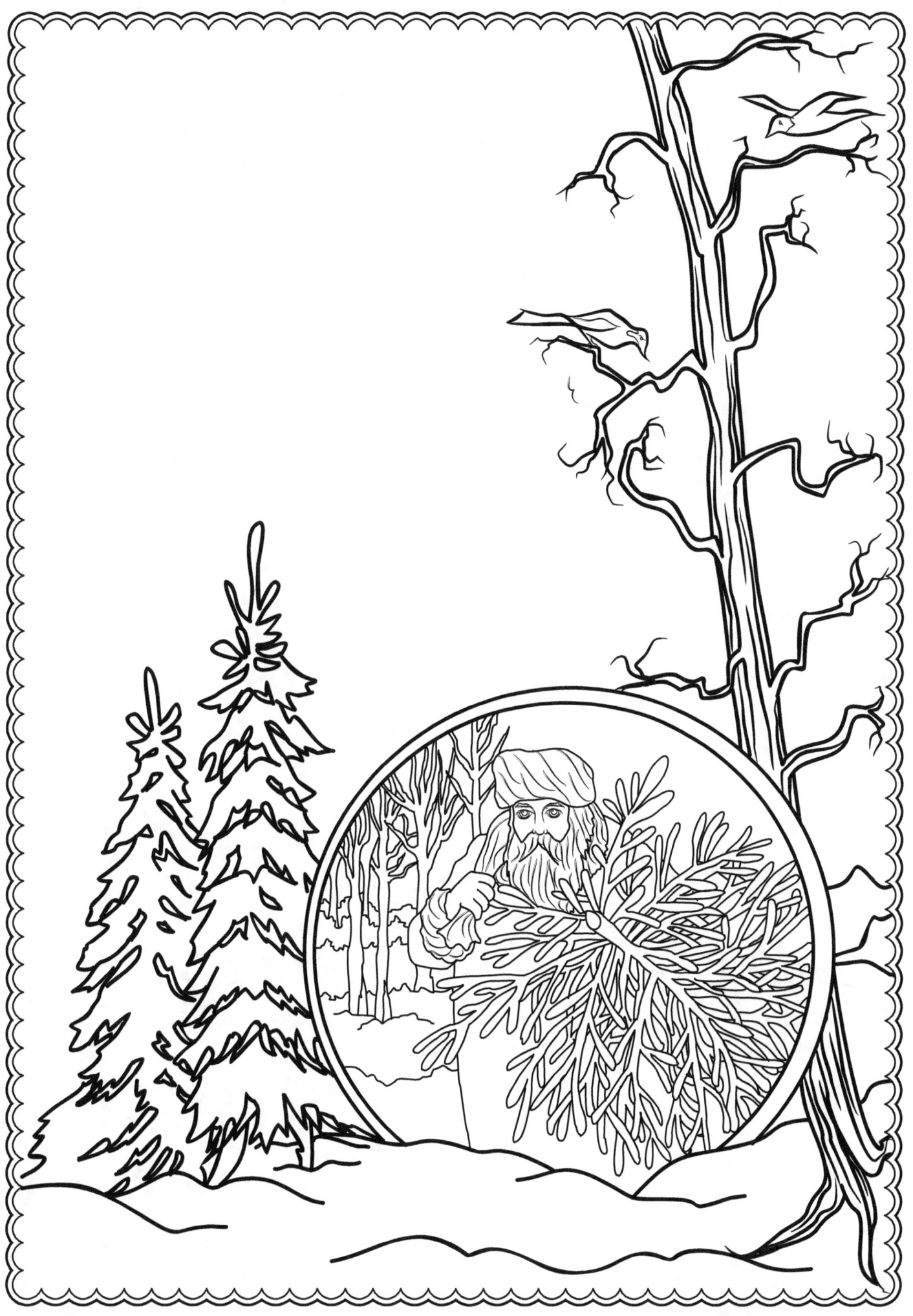

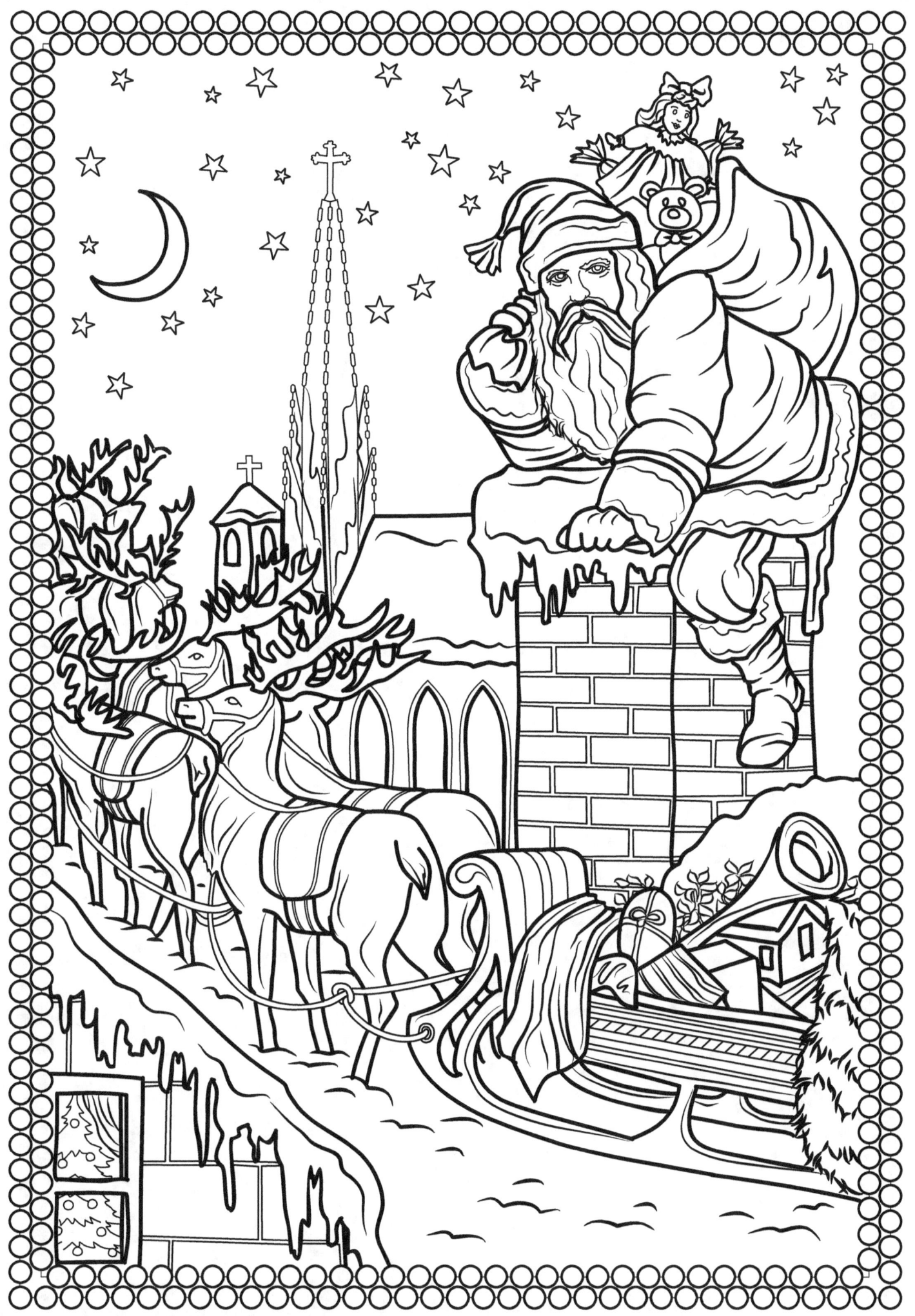

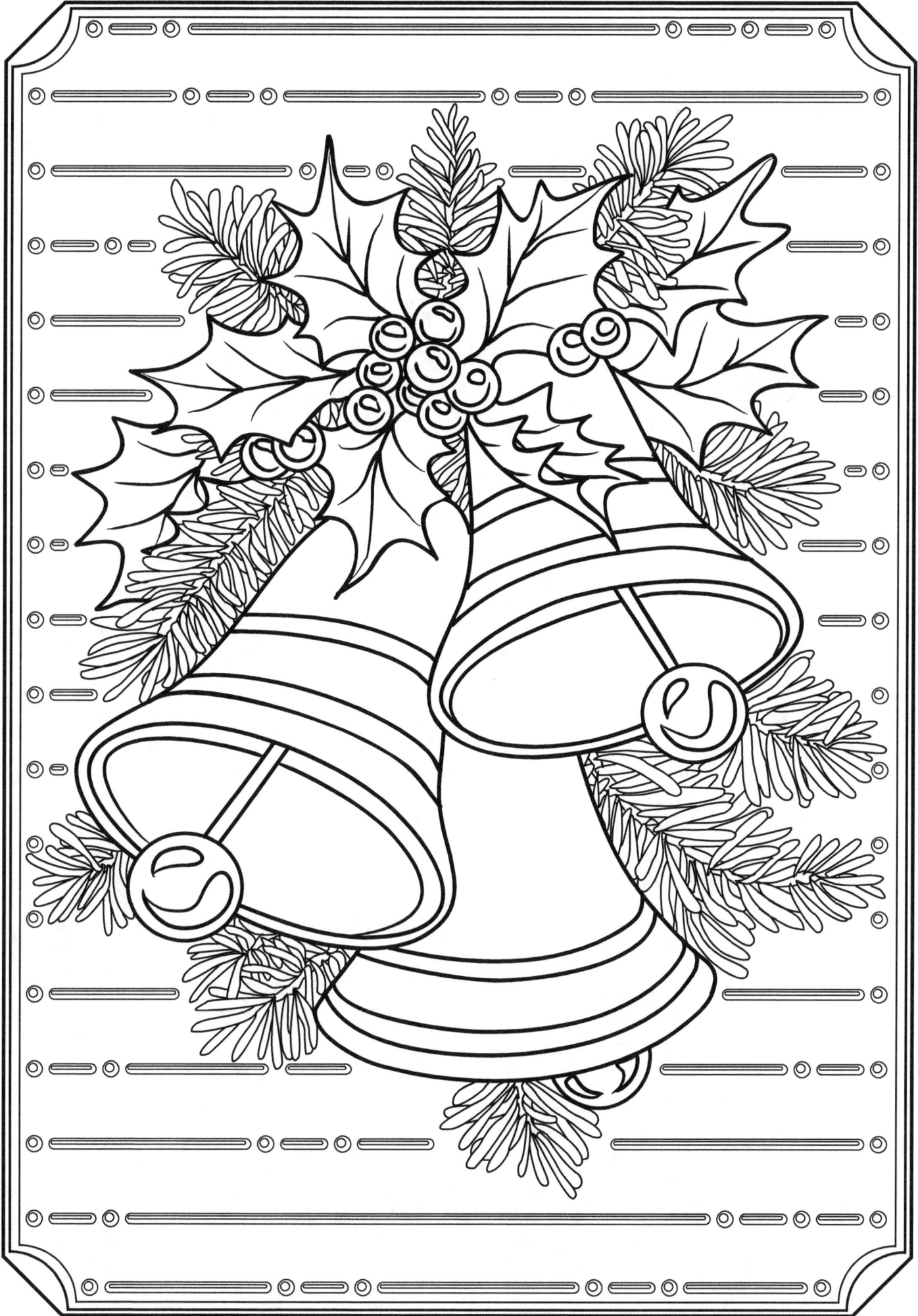

ArtworkAnywhere.com

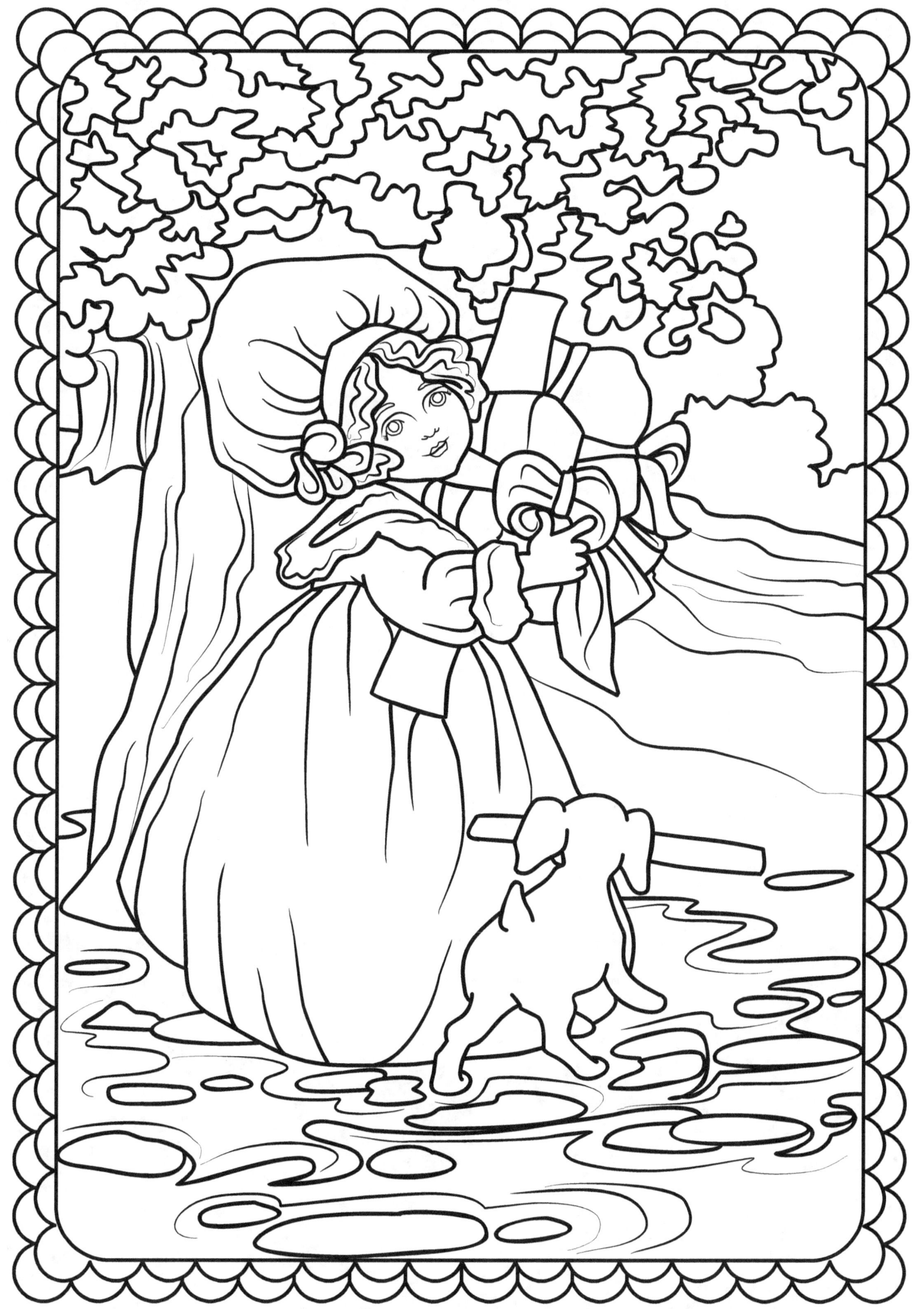

ArtworkAnywhere.com

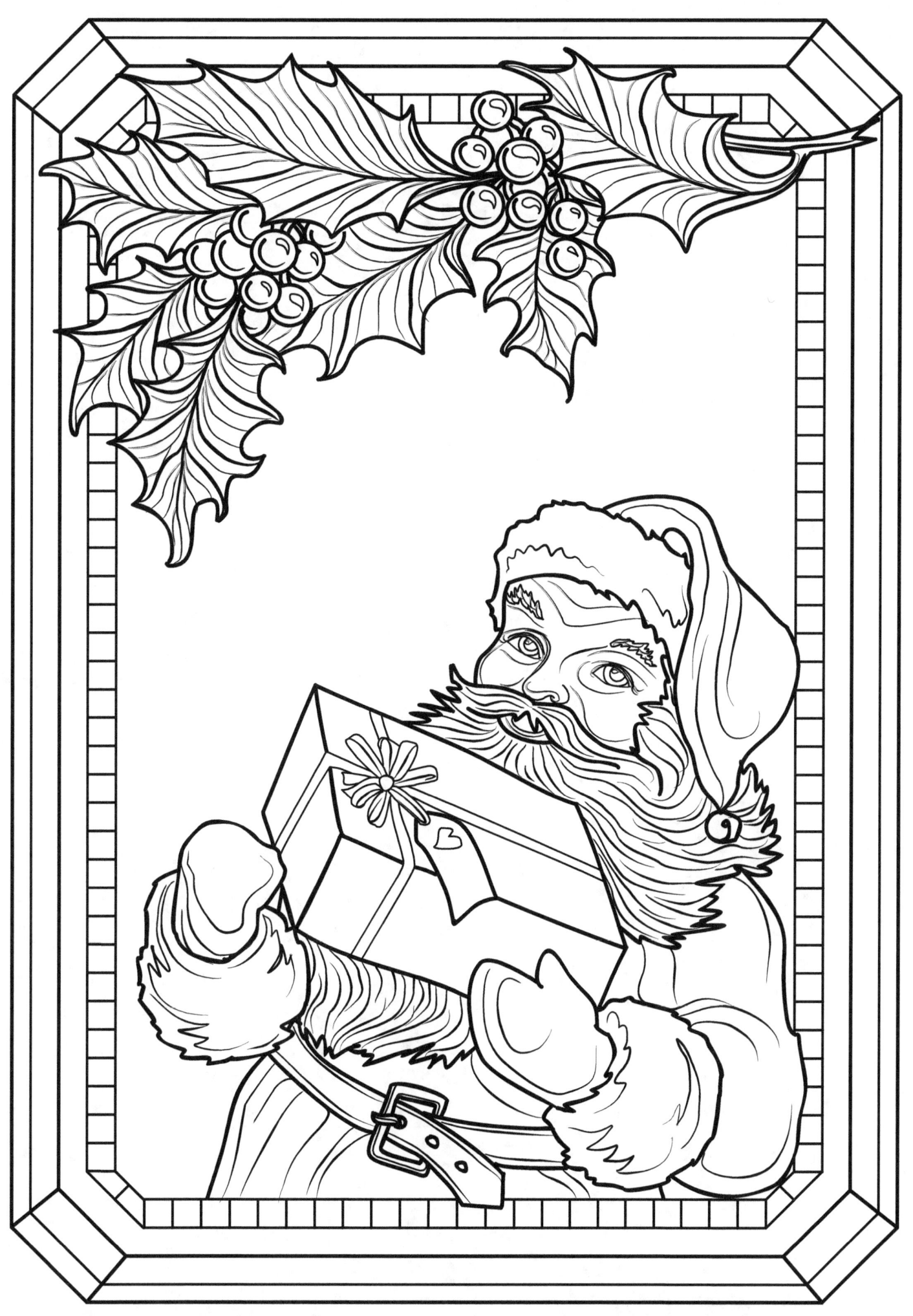

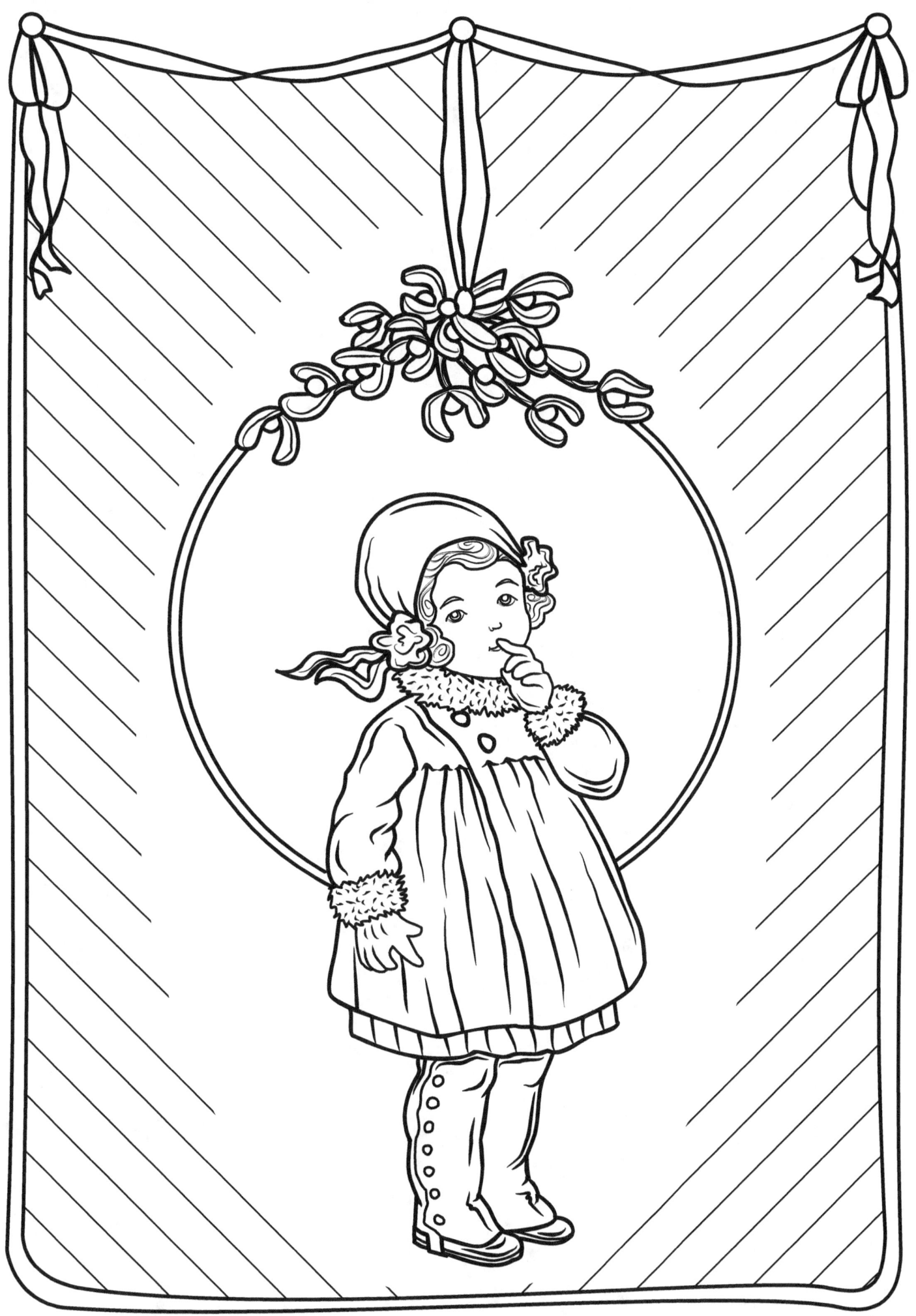

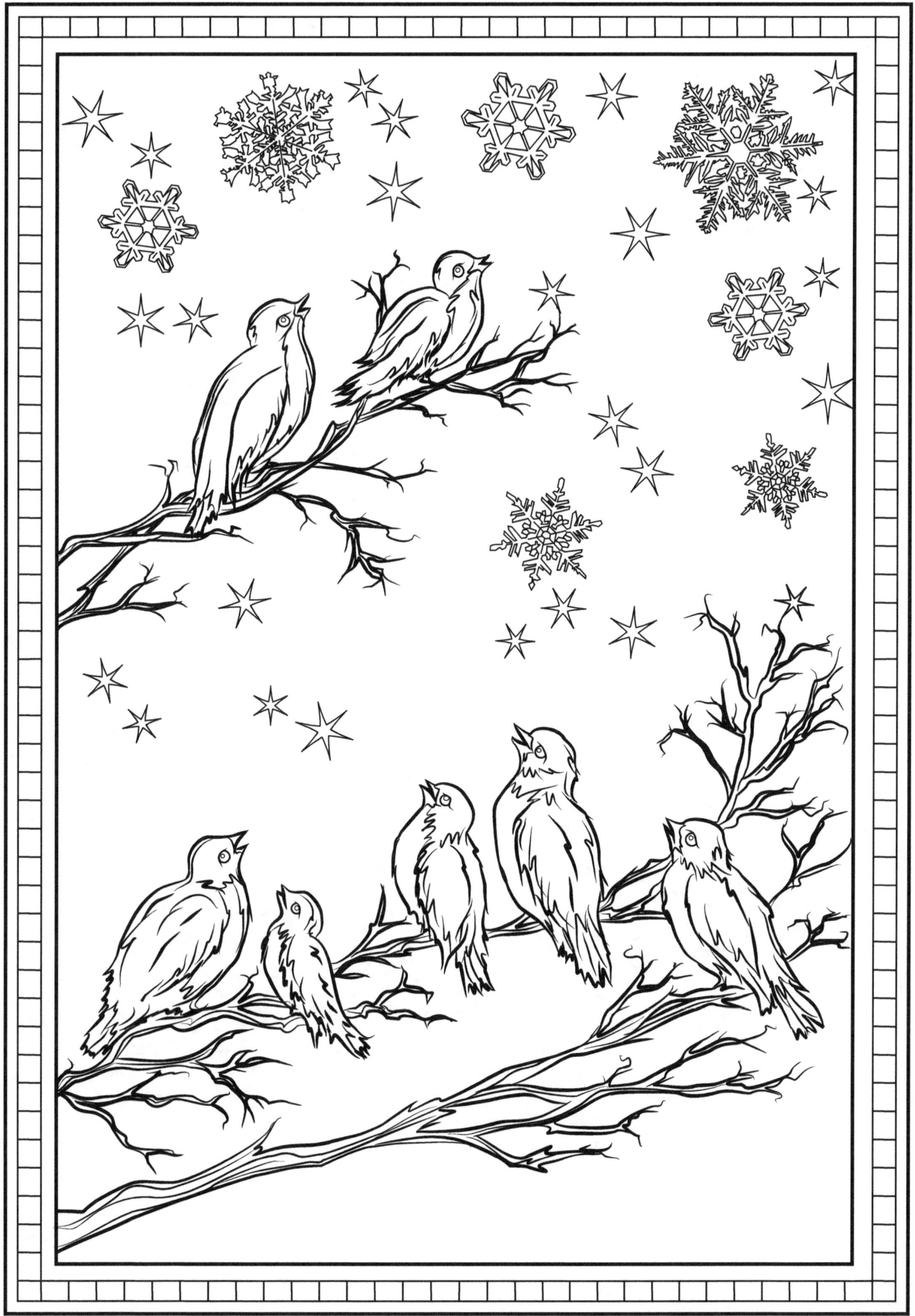

ArtworkAnywhere.com

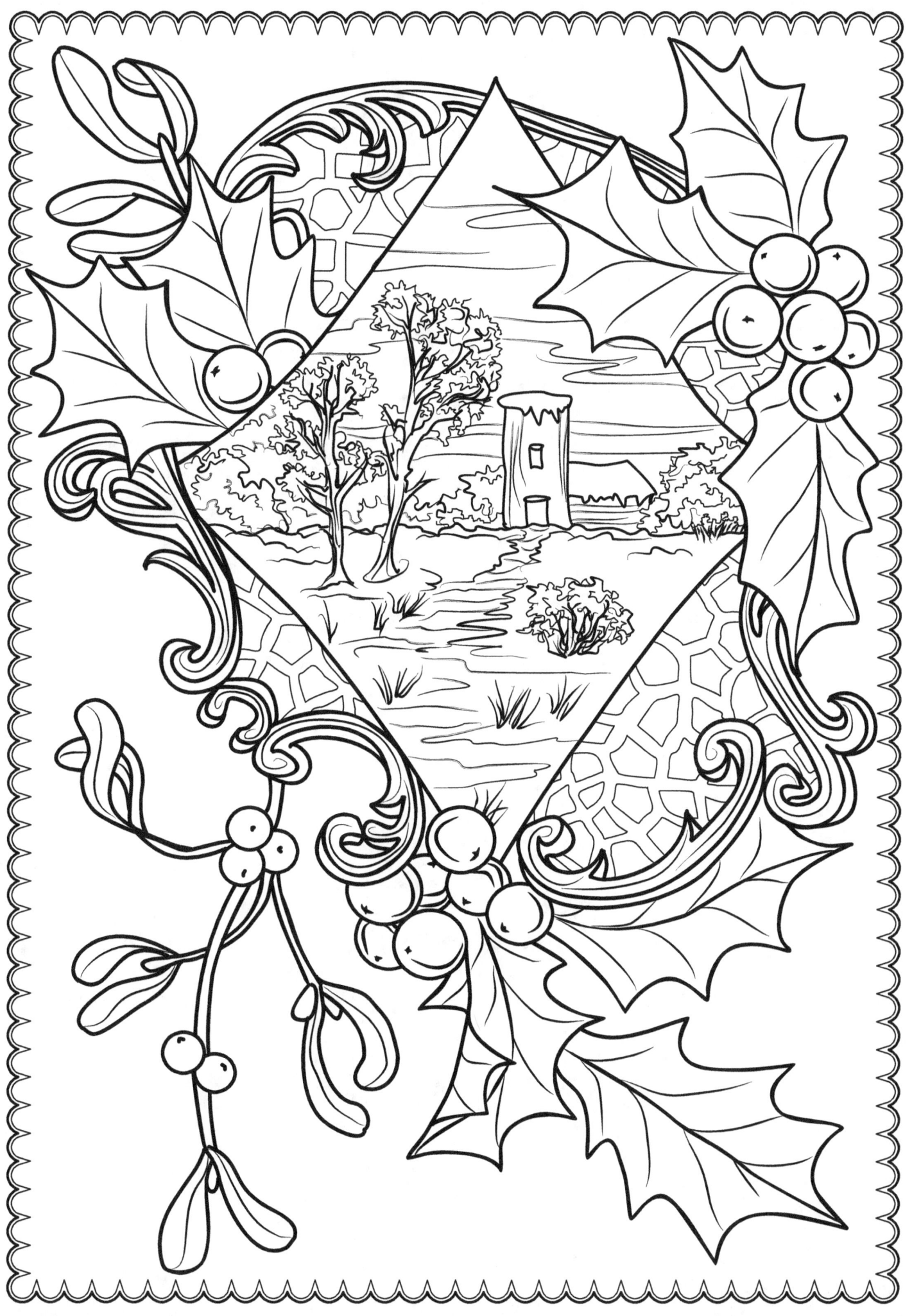

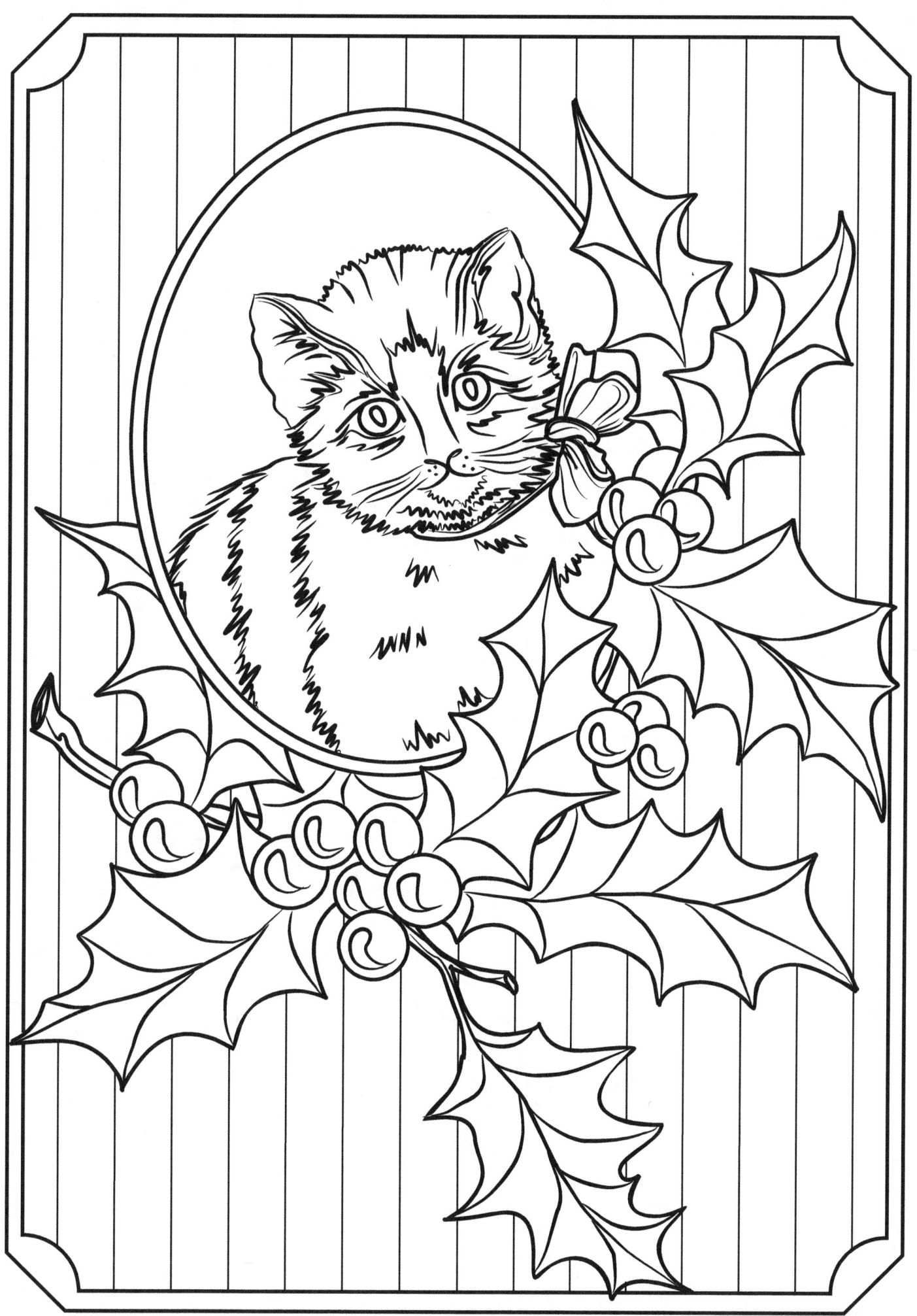

ArtworkAnywhere.com

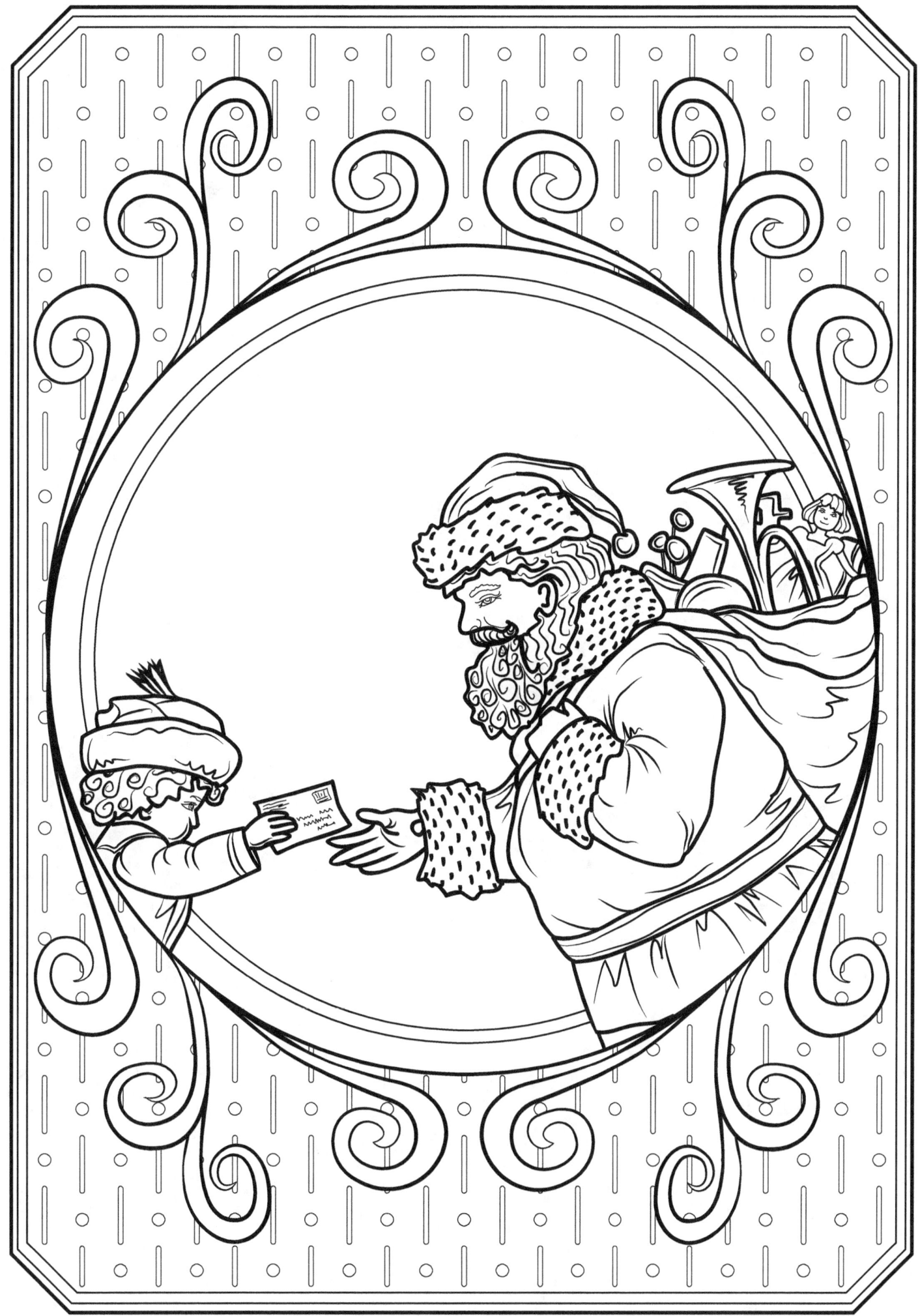

ArtworkAnywhere.com

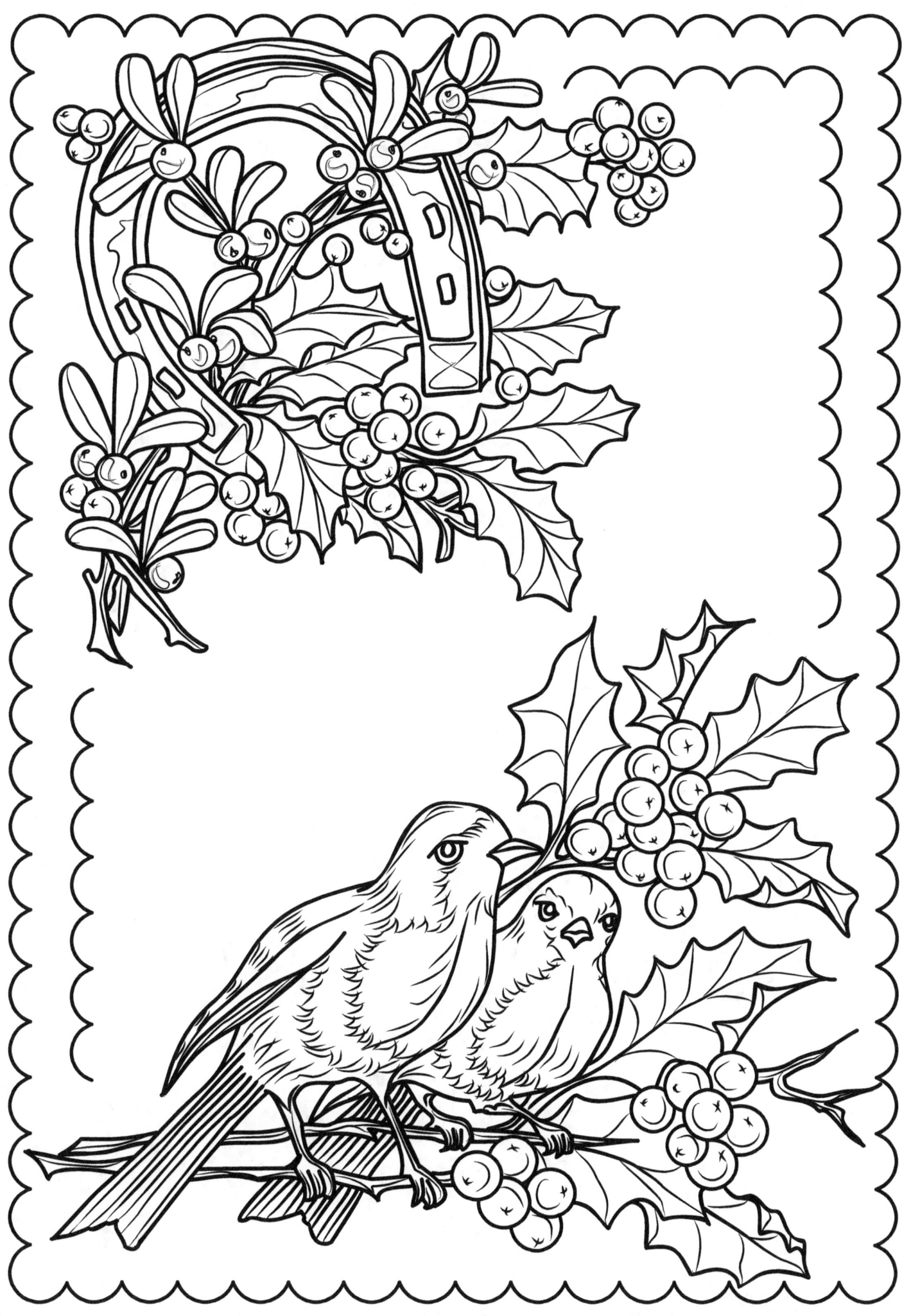

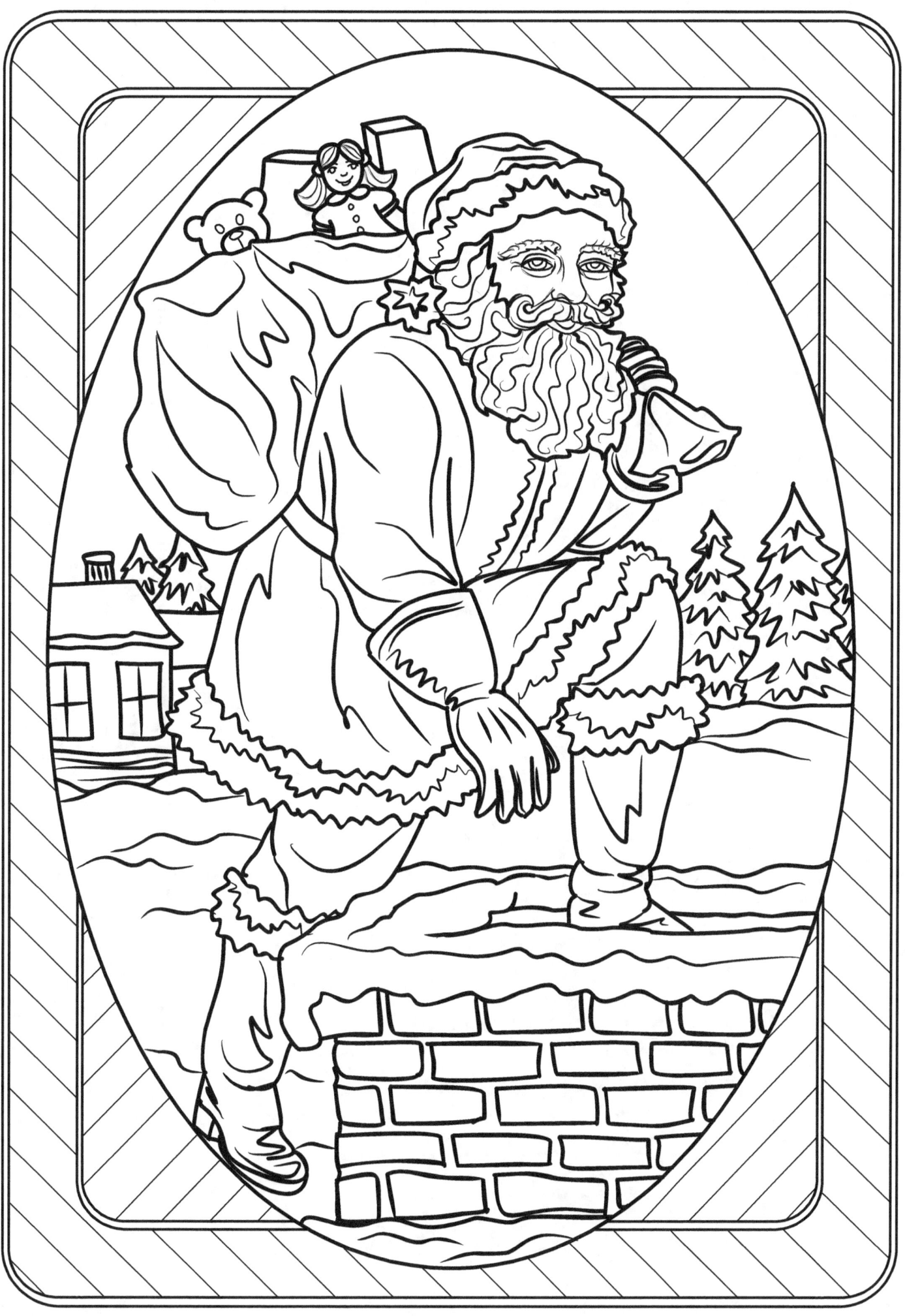

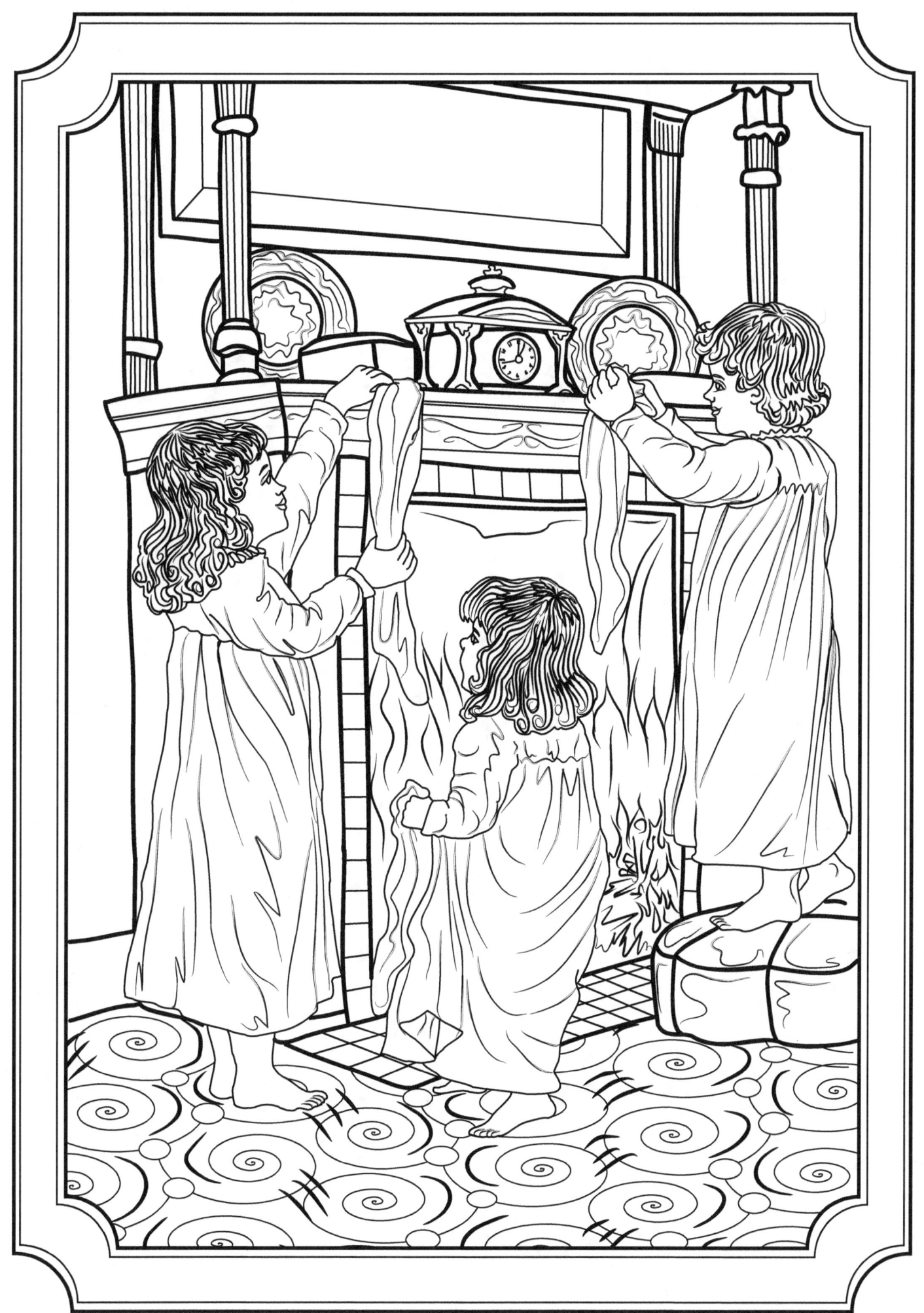

ArtworkAnywhere.com

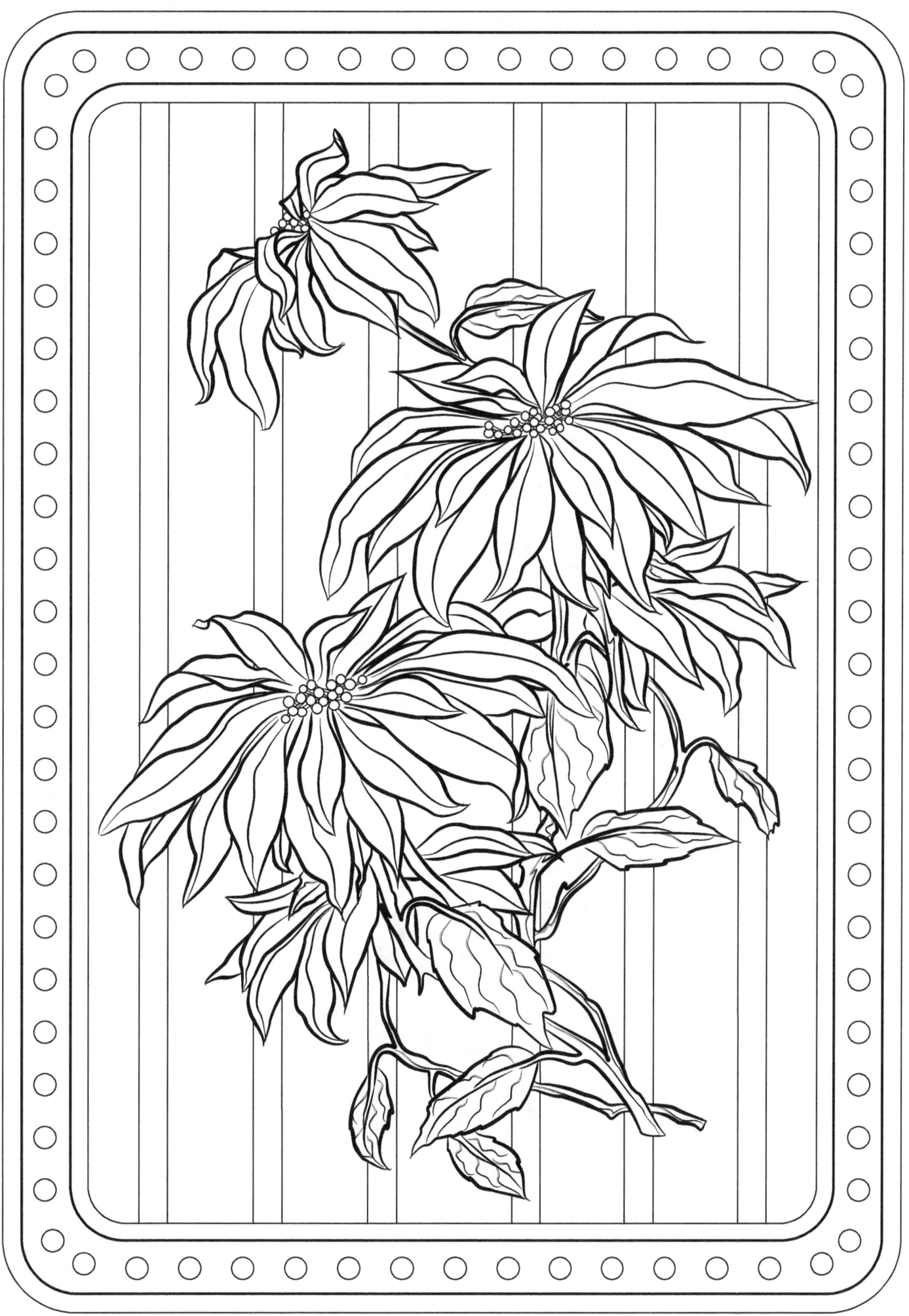

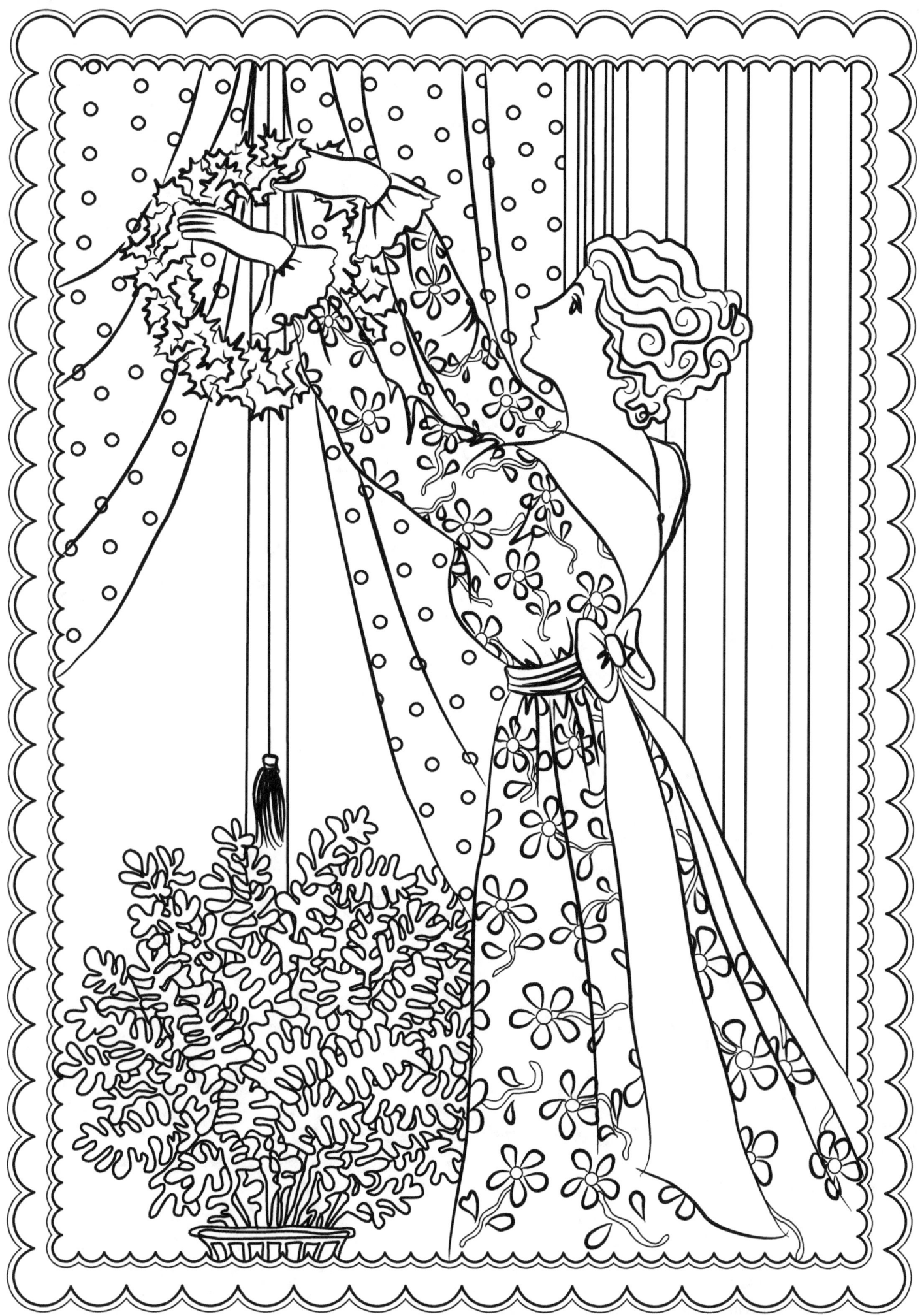

ArtworkAnywhere.com